LANGUAGE ARTS
WORKBOOK

4th Grade Semester A

Table of Contents

Module 1 1

Module 2 3

Module 3 11

Module 4 17

Module 5 21

Module 6 26

This workbook contains all of the worksheets that can be found in the Language Arts (ELA) 4A course. Students are expected to submit all completed work to his or her teacher.

© 2020 by Accelerate Education
Visit us on the Web at: www.accelerate.education

Student Name:

How Do You Read?

Directions: Select the answers that describe how you read below--even if you know it's not the best way to read. You can select more than one answer per question.

1. When I start reading a novel, I

>find page 1 and start reading.
>look at the table of contents to see if there are chapter titles.
>read the last page first.
>check to see if there are any pictures in the book.

2. When I read a section in a textbook, I

>read the subheadings and look at the picture first.
>read enough to answer the questions at the end of the section.
>read all paragraphs carefully and take notes.
>skim each section looking for main ideas.

3. For me, reading is like

>escaping into my own little world.
>having a tooth filled.
>taking a journey.
>doing the dishes.

4. When I don't understand something that I read, I usually

>stop reading and do something else.
>go back a few paragraphs or pages and reread.
>ask a classmate to explain what's happening.
>ask a teacher for help.

5. When I read for fun, I choose

>novels.
>magazines or non-fiction books.
>web sites.
>comic books.
>manga.
>poetry.

How Do You Read?

6. The place where I like to read is

    in my room.
    in the car or on the bus.
    outside.
    anywhere.

7. The best time for me to read is

    early morning.
    during school hours.
    before bed.
    any time.

8. To help myself remember what I read, I usually

    talk to other people about what I read.
    read things two or three times.
    take notes on what I read.
    summarize what I read--either in writing or out loud.

9. When I read a book or story that I really like, I

    look for other books by the same author.
    tell my friends or parents about the book.
    read the book or story again.
    try to write a similar story.

10. For me, the hardest part of reading is

    figuring out what new words mean.
    reading fast enough.
    remembering what I read.
    finding enough time to read.
    finding something that I like to read.
    making myself keep reading.
    something else:

Student Name:

Reading Goals

Directions: Select the answers that describe your style and interests. You can select more than one answer per question. At the end, fill out your reading goals for Semester 1.

---

1. What kinds of books do you like to read?

    fantasy (magic or fairy tale)
    stories about animals
    mysteries
    scary stories
    science fiction
    (the future or other worlds)
    realistic stories about kids your age
    true stories about real people
    books about how things work
    books that teach you how to do things
    books about other times in history
    other kinds of books:

2. What kinds of books would you like to try out from the list above?

3. Do you have any favorite authors?

    yes
    no

    If you do have favorite authors, write their names (or the titles of their books) here:

4. How long can you read in one sitting?

    15 minutes
    30 minutes
    about an hour
    more than an hour
    many hours

5. How many chapter books or novels do you usually read in a month?

    0
    1
    2
    3
    more than 3

....

My Reading Goals for Semester 1

1. I will read these kinds of books:

2. I will be able to read for   in one sitting.

3. I will read   books this semester.

4. The first two books I will read are:

Student Name:

Novel Plots

Directions: As you read your first novel of the semester, type or write down the answers to these questions. Keep this paper or file in a safe place so you can look at it during discussion with your teacher or classmates.

1. Describe the main problem in the novel you are reading.

2. How do the characters attempt to solve the main problem?

3. What conflicts occur in the novel as characters try to solve the main problem?

4. How is the novel's main problem resolved?

Module 2 - Reading Plot

Student Name:

Conflict in Novels

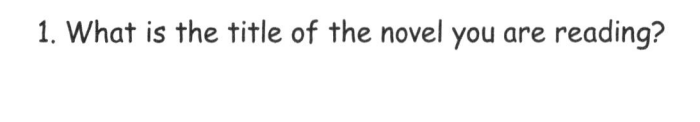

1. What is the title of the novel you are reading?

2. What is the main problem in the novel you are reading?

3. What conflicts do the characters deal with so far in your novel?

   Are the conflicts external or internal?

Student Name:

Ideas for Your Short Story

Try answering these questions to get some ideas for your story. If you answer them all, you're sure to get at least one good story idea!

1. What places have you visited that would make a good setting for a short story?

2. Find an interesting photograph of when you were younger. What was happening in your life when the picture was taken?

3. When have you been really scared or surprised? What event caused you to feel that way?

4. What activities are you really good at?

5. What subjects do you know a lot about?

6. Now that you've written down some details from your own life, think about a problem that someone (a short story character) might face, related to a place, time, event, or activity in your life. Describe that problem here:

Ideas for Your Short Story

Brainstorming Using Pictures

Use each picture to help you think of an idea for a problem that a character might try to solve in a story. Write your idea next to the picture.

Ideas for Your Short Story

Now, choose one of your ideas and think about it some more. Fill in the story map below with ideas for your story's characters, setting, problem, and conflict.

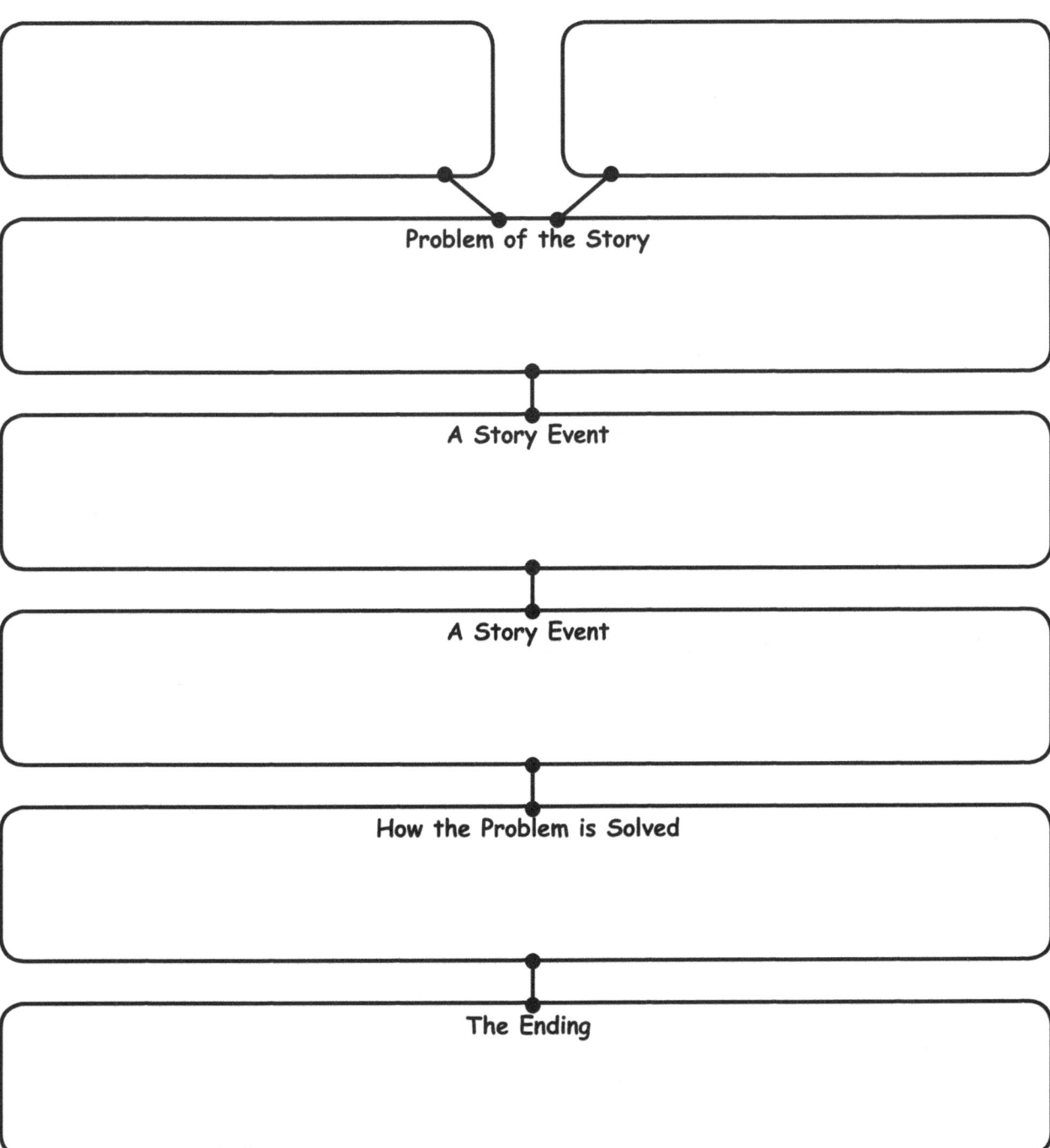

Module 2 - Writing Problems

Student Name:

Practice Using Relative Adverbs

Directions: Complete each of these sentences by adding details after the relative adverb.

1. The best place to see the sunset is where . . .

2. I like to go swimming when . . .

3. Television is the reason why . . .

Directions: Write a sentence using one of the relative adverbs *where*, *why*, or *when*.

Be sure to check your answers and look for mistakes!

Module 2 - Writing Problems

Student Name:

Build Your Story's Setting

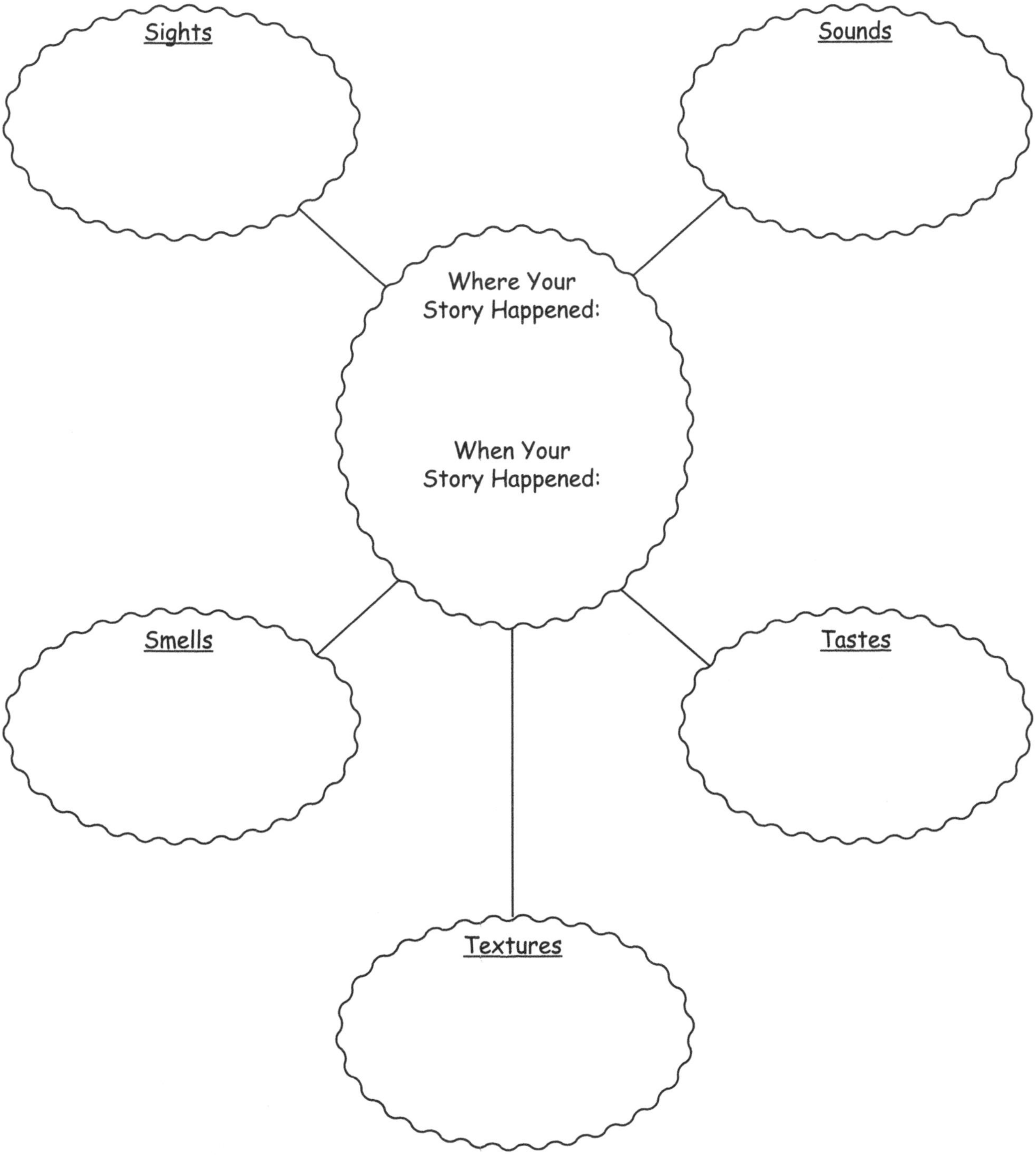

Sights

Sounds

Where Your Story Happened:

When Your Story Happened:

Smells

Tastes

Textures

Module 2 - Writing Setting

Student Name:

Develop Your Characters

My Main Character:

1. Describe what your main character looks like:

2. What does your main character like, or like to do?

3. Describe your main character's personality.

4. Make up something that your character did that shows a character trait.

5. What kinds of things might your character say?

Be sure to check your answers and look for mistakes!

Student Name:

Novel Characters

Your Novel:

List two of the main characters in your novel:

Name of Character 1:

Character Traits:

Name of Character 2:

Character Traits:

Be sure to check your answers and look for mistakes!

Student Name:

Writing Dialogue

What two people or characters will speak to each other for your dialogue?

What do you want to show about each character?

Character 1	Character 2
Character Traits:	Character Traits:

What situation or topic will your characters talk about?

Write your dialogue in the space below. Remember to include your characters' actions as well as their words.

Student Name:

Practice Punctuating Dialogue

Directions: Add the needed punctuation marks to this dialogue. Then check your work using the answer key.

How did you get your new puppy? Phillip asked. He's cute, but he's huge!

We stopped by the pound on the way home from school answered Maria.

Phillip looked confused. They charged you by the pound? he asked. That sounds expensive!

No said Maria, laughing. We got him at the pound. You know, it's like the SPCA. You go there to rescue stray animals.

Oh I get it now said Phillip. So, how much did he weigh?

Be sure to check your answers and look for mistakes!

Module 3 - Dialogue   14

Student Name:

Relative Pronouns Practice

Directions: Finish each sentence using a clause (sentence part) that begins with a relative pronoun (who, whom, whoever, whomever, what, which, or that).

1. Dwayne said, "I would like to be friends with someone . . .

2. If she had a million dollars, she would share it with . . .

3. Beatrice wanted the kind of dog . . .

4. When the boys saw the mess in the garage, they wondered . . .

5. I knew that one day I would find . . .

Be sure to check your answers and look for mistakes!

Student Name:

Choose Your Narrator

1. Who is the main character in the narrative you will write?
   (If the story is about something that happened to you, then you are the main character.)

2. Who will tell the story?
   (Who will be the narrator?)

   the main character
   another character besides the main character
   someone who wasn't involved in the story

3. What point of view will your story have?

   first person (I.....)
   third-person (He/she.....)

4. Now that you've selected a narrator and point of view, practice using that point of view to tell the story. Look back at your prewriting notes for your story. Then write either the first paragraph or an important scene in the story.

Module 3 - Writing Point of View

Student Name:

Who's Your Narrator?

1. Is the narrator of your story also one of its characters? If so, who is it?

2. How old is your narrator?

3. How much does your narrator know about what's going to happen in your story? Everything? Just what he or she experienced?

4. Will your narrator know how the characters feel or what they think? Or will your narrator be more limited?

5. Does your narrator have a particular reason for telling the story?

6. How does your narrator feel about the people or what happens in your story?

Be sure to check your answers and look for mistakes!

17 Module 4 - Introducing Narrators

Student Name:

Practice Punctuating Quotes

This paragraph is from the novel *Black Beauty*, a novel narrated by a horse with that name. Here Black Beauty describes his first master.

Our master was a good, kind man. He gave us good food, good lodging, and kind words; he spoke as kindly to us as he did to his little children. We were all fond of him, and my mother loved him very much. When she saw him at the gate she would neigh with joy, and trot up to him. He would play and stroke her and say, "Well, old Pet, and how is your little Darkie?" I was a dull black, so he called me Darkie; then he would give me a piece of bread, which was very good, and sometimes he brought a carrot for my mother. All the horses would come to him, but I think we were his favorites. My mother always took him to the town on a market day in a light gig.

Directions: Add any needed punctuation marks to these sentences about the narrator of Black Beauty.

1. Black Beauty's first master was very kind--he gave his horses good food, good lodging, and kind words. He treated his horses like his children.

2. Black Beauty probably learned to trust humans since his first master was kind and his mother loved him very much.

3. The narrator's master taught his horses to think of treats when they see humans. The narrator says that the master "would give me a piece of bread, which was very good, and sometimes he brought a carrot for my mother. The way the narrator talks about his human master makes the reader like him too.

4. The novel's narrator seems to think very highly of himself. When he talks about his master, he says all the horses would come to him, but I think we were his favorites. He thinks this because his mother got to pull their master to town on market day.

Be sure to check your answers and look for mistakes!

Module 4 - Using Direct Quotes

Student Name:

Finding Themes in Novels

Directions: Use the steps below to find at least one theme in a novel you have read (or one you're reading right now).

1. Describe one of the main problems in the novel. What are the novel's main characters up against?

2. Explain how this problem is solved. What do the characters do to solve the problem?

3. Describe how the main characters develop throughout the novel. What do the characters learn? How do they change?

4. Connect these changes or lessons to life. What does the story say about what life is like-- or what it means to be human?

Be sure to check your answers and look for mistakes!

19   Module 4 - Describing Themes

Student Name:

Writing Themes

Directions: Use the questions below to write a short paragraph describing a theme in your novel.

Your Novel:

1. Look back at your Finding Themes in Novels worksheet. Copy your answers to question #4 in the space below.

2. Write a sentence that starts out "One theme in the novel is . . ." In the second part of the sentence, write the theme you copied down in question #1 above.

3. Copy your sentence from question #2 in the space below. Then add a sentence that describes what happens in the novel to show the theme you found.

4. Look back at the examples of good theme statements from the lesson. Revise your theme statement so that it is easy to read and understand, and make sure it has the two parts it needs to be a good theme statement.

Be sure to check your answers and look for mistakes!

Module 4 - Describing Themes   20

Student Name:

Finding Common Themes

Directions: Answer these questions as you reread "The Fisherman and His Wife" and "The Gift of the Little People."

1. Which of these themes is common to both stories?

    the importance of friendship

    how unreliable magic is--you can't count on it

    power makes people behave badly

2. Write a sentence saying that the two stories share the theme you checked in the list above. (This is your claim.)

3. Write two reasons why you believe the stories share this theme.

4. Describe at least one detail from each story that supports each of the reasons you wrote.

Be sure to check your answers and look for mistakes!

21   Module 5 - Common Themes

Make a Claim

1. Which story do you want to write about?

    ☐ "The Talkative Turtle"

    ☐ "The Gold in the Orchard"

2. What's your opinion? Is this story a good way to pass along the culture's beliefs and values?

3. What's your opinion? Should this story's message get taught to children?

4. Make a claim. Choose one of your opinions (your answer to #2 or #3). Write your opinion like this:

"The Talkative Turtle" is/is not a good way to pass along beliefs and values.

or

Children should/should not be taught the message of "The Gold in the Orchard."

WRITE YOUR CLAIM HERE: (Make sure that your claim says *your* opinion.)

5. Now write some reasons to back up your claim. What are your reasons for thinking the way you do about how these little stories are used?

    1.

    2.

    3.

6. Copy your reasons into this chart. For each reason, give an example from the story to explain your reason.

	Your Reasons	**Examples from the Story**
1		
2		
3		

7. Now write your claim and your reasons as an essay or paper. (You can copy and paste your sentences below, or you can write your essay on notebook paper--then scan it and send it to your teacher.)

Use this list of sentences as a guide.

Sentence #1: Your claim

Sentence #2: Your first reason

Sentence #3: Your example for the first reason

Sentence #4: Your second reason

Sentence #5: Your example for the second reason

Sentence #6: Your third reason

Sentence #7: Your example for the third reason

Student Name:

Paraphrase It

1. Paraphrase **Multimedia Message #1** in the space below. What does the video clip say about why it's important to take care of forests?

2. Paraphrase **Multimedia Message #2** in the space below. What does the presentation say about humans as a species?

3. Paraphrase part of **Multimedia Message #3** in the space below. What does the narrator say about why Sequoyah created a written Cherokee language?

Be sure to check your answers and look for mistakes!

Module 5 - Paraphrasing Multimedia

Student Name:

Tag It

Write or copy and paste your opinion essay here (the current version of it):

Now, rewrite your opinion essay with transitional tags added in at least three places. Underline the transitional tags you added--or change the font of these words to boldface, so your teacher can see what you added.

Be sure to check your answers and look for mistakes!

25   Module 5 - Transitions

Student Name:

Analyze This

1. Who are the characters in the story?

2. Who is the main character?

3. What is the story's setting?

4. What setting details are most important?

5. What events make up the plot? (List them in order.)

6. How would the story be different if the events happened in a different order?

Be sure to check your answers and look for mistakes!

Module 6 - Multimedia Stories

Student Name:

Analyze Stereotypes

1. Who are the characters in the story? What groups do they belong to?
   (Examples of groups include men, American Indian, and elderly or senior citizens.)

List characters here.	What group does each character belong to?

2. How do the characters in the story behave? What are they like?

List characters here.	How do they act? What are they like?

3. Look at the behaviors listed in the right column above. Do all people in those groups act that way? If not, the character may be a stereotype.

List characters here.	Is this character a stereotype?

Be sure to check your answers and look for mistakes!

Student Name:

Peer Review Worksheet

Your Peer's Name:

1. Read your peer's story. If you were able to print out a copy, make notes on the page about parts that you like. Also mark any parts that you didn't understand or had questions about.

2. After you finish reading the story, think about how the story made you feel. Did it make you laugh, feel angry, or feel sad? Were parts of the story scary or suspenseful? In the space below, write some notes about how the story affected you.

3. Look back at the parts of the story that you liked most. Describe those parts here, and explain why you liked them.

4. Think about what would make the story more interesting or successful. Write down two or three suggestions for the writer. Things you might suggest include sections to add details or sections to move to another place in the story.

5. Did you have any questions about the story? Was there any part that you didn't understand? If so, write those questions in the space below.

Student Name:

Researching Narcissus

Directions: Type the word Narcissus into an internet search engine if you have access to the internet and are allowed to do an internet search. If not, look up Narcissus in an encyclopedia or a book about Greek mythology. When you have found a reference, answer the questions below.

1. Who is/was Narcissus?

2. What character traits of the mythological character are shared by the main character in the cartoon?

3. What happens in the original myth?

4. How is the "modern spin" on Narcissus like the original?

5. How is the "modern spin" different from the original?

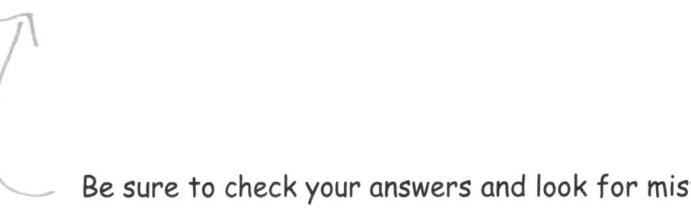 Be sure to check your answers and look for mistakes!

29   Module 6 - Using References

Student Name:

Comparing Cat Myths

Watch the first video, Egyptian Worship of Cats. As you watch the video, fill in the middle column of the chart below. If there is no information in the video about one of the questions, leave that row blank. (Also, you don't need to use complete sentences--you're just taking notes for this assignment.)

	Egyptian Mythology	Asian Mythology
What powers do cats have in each mythology?		
What do cats symbolize, or stand for?		
What did cats bring to the people?		
What did cats do to hurt people?		
What myths has the culture passed down, related to cats?		
Describe what happens in the culture's cat myth.		

Now watch the second video, The Cult of the Super-Predator. As you watch the video, fill in the last column of the chart. If there is no information in the video about one of the questions, leave that row blank.

When you have written down everything important in the videos, send this worksheet to your teacher AND save a copy to use later in the lesson.

Be sure to check your answers and look for mistakes!

Module 6 - Creation Myths

Student Name:

Comparing Horse Myths

Watch the first video, The Kelpie. As you watch the video, fill in the middle column of the chart below. If there is no information in the video about one of the questions, leave that row blank. (Also, you don't need to use complete sentences--you're just taking notes for this assignment.)

	Scottish Mythology	Greek Mythology
In the culture's myths, where does the horse come from?		
What does the horse symbolize, or stand for?		
What do horses do to help people?		
What do horses do to hurt people?		
What myths has the culture passed down, related to horses?		
Describe what happens in the culture's horse myth.		

Now watch the second video, Horses and the Sea. As you watch the video, fill in the last column of the chart. If there is no information in the video about one of the questions, leave that row blank.

When you have written down everything important in the videos, send this worksheet to your teacher AND save a copy to use later in the lesson.

Be sure to check your answers and look for mistakes!

31 Module 6 - Creation Myths

Student Name:

Comparing Dragon Myths

Watch the first video, The Chinese View of Dragons. As you watch the video, fill in the middle column of the chart below. If there is no information in the video about one of the questions, leave that row blank. (Also, you don't need to use complete sentences--you're just taking notes for this assignment.)

	Chinese Mythology	Christian Mythology
How do the people in this culture feel about dragons?		
What does the dragon symbolize, or stand for?		
What do dragons do to help people?		
What do dragons do to hurt people?		
What myths has the culture passed down, related to dragons?		
Describe what happens in the culture's dragon myth.		

Now watch the second video, The Christian View of Dragons. As you watch the video, fill in the last column of the chart. If there is no information in the video about one of the questions, leave that row blank.

When you have written down everything important in the videos, send this worksheet to your teacher AND save a copy to use later in the lesson.

Be sure to check your answers and look for mistakes!

Module 6 - Creation Myths

32

© 2021 by Accelerate Education
Visit us on the Web at: www.accelerate.education
ISBN: 978-1-63916-020-4